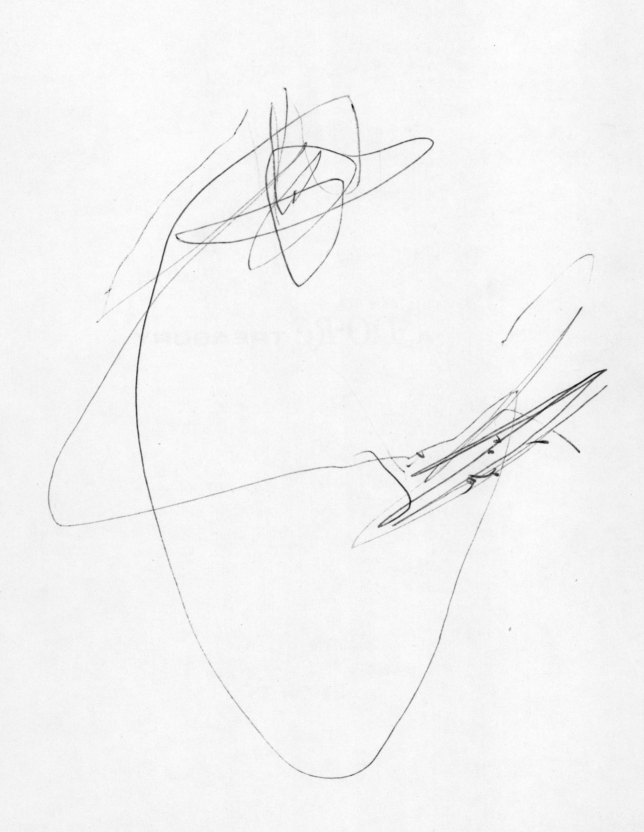

A DORÉ TREASURY

A DORÉ
TREASURY

A COLLECTION OF THE BEST ENGRAVINGS

OF GUSTAVE DORÉ

edited and with an introduction by JAMES STEVENS

Bounty Books   A DIVISION OF CROWN PUBLISHERS, INC.

THE INCREDIBLE GUSTAVE DORÉ

FOR MOST OF US, GENIUS IS CONTEMPLATED with awe and fascination. We have grown accustomed to a pattern: extraordinary people struggling against every type of difficulty to bring early promise and talent to that state of near-perfection we call genius—and then frequently frustrated in having that talent recognized. Indeed, the pattern has led us to believe that struggle is a prerequisite for genius.

But the genius of Gustave Doré, perhaps the most popular worldwide illustrator of the latter half of the nineteenth century and certainly a master draftsman and artist for all ages, took a completely different course. His was a strange, eerie, and wholly astounding kind of talent. He never struggled for either perfection of technique or recognition. He could draw long before he could write, and even in his childhood drawings nobody could miss his incredible capacity for rich detail or the control he exercised over his work, which would have done many an adult credit. His technical capacities were recognized professionally by the time he was fifteen, when he began to earn a comfortable living as an artist. His facility, together with an imagination as weird and yet as true and profound as his talent, made him an international celebrity not long after he was twenty.

Strangely enough, Doré's imagination, the crux of his genius and universality, seems to have developed in much the same way as did his technical abilities. It was always there, from earliest childhood, and never really seemed to change much—at least not in spirit— even long after he had become an adult. His very last works are filled with the qualities of children's daydreams, with the grotesqueries of his earliest and least inhibited fantasies, and layered with the surrealistic qualities found only in the best folk and fairy tales. Indeed, there are many critics who claim that Doré's genius was a direct result of his remaining, emotionally, at least, a child. For it is true that in many ways the irrepressible Doré, as extraordinary as a man as he was as an artist, never really grew up. His personal attractiveness, charm, and easy talent had made him a spoiled, but nonetheless delightful, brat of a child. Perhaps these same qualities, which he retained as an adult, made it unnecessary for Doré ever really to change.

If there is nothing in Doré's background—aside from his early clutching of the pencil—to indicate a born artist, there is much to explain the strange humor and imagination that are the hallmarks of his art. He was born Paul Gustave Doré, on January 6, 1833, in Strasbourg, Alsace-Lorraine. His father, a practical man, was the engineer of roads and bridges for the Alsatian district, and the tiny house in which they lived, and where Doré was born, lay in the shadow of Strasbourg's Cathedral, a great medieval structure. It was one of the first sights young Gustave remembered ever seeing, and its gloomy, gothic grandeur was to remain in his memory, and in his drawing style, to the end of his days. He was always attracted to structures and natural phenomena that were mysteriously gloomy, with a strange air about them, and, as with all of his illustrations, with some underlying terror that is nevertheless impelling in spite of its scariness. One of his favorite places as a child, for example, was the Black Forest, which he visited with his father. Since Alsace-Lorraine borders on both France and Germany—and has belonged to both at various moments in history—Gustave was treated to some spectacular views of both nations.

The truth is that although considered both a Frenchman and French artist, Gustave Doré did not escape the German part of his Alsatian heritage. There is, in his nearly every illustration and drawing from childhood on, that frighteningly bitter, surrealistic gloom that pervades most German literature and, more importantly, German folklore, myth, and fairy tale. In no area of drawing would Doré prove himself better at capturing, with even a single illustration, the very essence of a myth, whether it stemmed from classical literature or the homespun poetry of the folk tale—but always with a touch of the bizarre, which lent to whatever story he illustrated both an underlying terror and a strange kind of humor that uniquely reinforced each other.

This coexistence of conscious irony and nightmarish bizarreness was a part of Doré's style even as a child, although he seemed to have an extraordinarily happy childhood. Exactly when he began to draw, Doré himself could not remember. His nurse, Francoise, does not remember him without a pencil past the age of four. Like a child asking that the damage to a favorite toy be repaired, he would run to his father, or his father's friends, to sharpen his pencil at both ends so that it would last longer.

Though it was clear from the first that Doré's talent was no ordinary one, the practical Papa Doré had no wish to indulge Gustave and allow him to pursue art as a profession. He wanted his son to be an engineer, and he tried everything to stop Gustave's preoccupation with art. He insisted that Gustave pay more attention to his schoolwork, for while the boy was certainly not dull, he was not exactly a model student. Mischief was his middle name, and he wreaked revenge on all the lessons he was made to read by caricaturing all of the stories and handing them in instead of his lessons. Fortunately for Gustave, his teachers were enlightened and rather pleased with his talent, and he managed his way through school very well, though he never did receive his bachelor's degree.

When Papa Doré found he could not influence Gustave away from his pencils, he tried ordering the boy not to touch them. But Gustave took so ill without pencil and paper that his father had to relent. Finally, in a last-ditch effort to turn Gustave from his drawing, Doré bought him a violin. Much to his dismay, Gustave fell in love with the violin and now filled the house with both his music and his drawings. His father could do nothing but insist that Gustave keep up his grades at school and not think of a career in art.

In 1847, for the first time, Gustave, then fifteen, visited Paris with his family. Once he had seen "the center of light and culture," as he called it, he was determined to remain there rather than return to Strasbourg with his parents. One day, after staring for some moments in the shopwindow of Auber and Philipon, it occurred to Gustave to "dash off a few caricatures" like those he had been looking at. He returned to his hotel, set to work, and, taking advantage of his parents' absence, brought the finished caricatures back to the well-known publishers. Philipon was immediately impressed. He managed to dispel Papa Doré's fears about a career in art, and offered Gustave a three-year contract at a generous salary. This would enable him to finish his education as well as remain in Paris, if Gustave would produce one lithograph cartoon per week for the new magazine Philipon was about to publish—the soon-to-be-celebrated *Journal pour Rire*.

Gustave worked hard for the next seven years. He did return to school, where he was adored by both students and teachers, although, as mentioned before, he managed to drop out of college before receiving his degree. He turned out a prodigious amount of work, and made the somewhat difficult switch from lithography to woodcuts. But by the eighteen fifties, the restless Doré was extremely discontented with what he called his "comic work." He wanted to illustrate *Rabelais*. After much effort, he succeeded in finding a publisher, and his *Rabelais* appeared in 1854. All of Paris was absolutely entranced. Avid readers of *Rabelais*, which they knew practically by heart, felt that Doré had actually brought them face to face with the familiar characters for the very first time. Coming from the French, this was much more than mere praise, and Gustave Doré, at age twenty-two, found himself established for all of his life as a sought-after and celebrated artist.

The rest, in terms of Doré's life as an illustrator, is history. In 1855, he illustrated Balzac's *Droll Stories*, in addition to many lesser-known works. In 1861, he illustrated Dante's *Inferno*, one of Doré's best-known works. In 1862 came the *Perrault Fairy Tales*, with all of Doré's penchant for the gothic and Black Forest eeriness, and the same year saw his illustrations for Rhin's *Mythology*, *The Adventures of Baron Munchausen*, and about five other books. Indeed, Doré's work which had always been prodigious would continue to remain so until the end of his days, and even Gustave himself could never quite keep track of the many thousands of illustrations he had created, except for those so famous and marvelous that none, having once seen them, could ever forget them. In 1863, Doré's *Don Quixote* appeared. The *Don Quixote* is especially important among Doré's works because it suggests another area of art in which Doré had become enormously interested—painting. Much of the quality in the Quixote illustrations, especially the lights and shades, depended greatly on painting technique. And it was the thorn in Doré's side that, while he might be amazingly successful in using these techniques in his illustrations, he had little success with his paintings.

Success had come so easily to him in his drawing, he could scarcely believe recognition would not come as quickly and easily for his painting. It was a black spot in what otherwise seemed to be a delightfully happy life. He began exhibiting his paintings, receiving either no notice or unfavorable notice. It made him rather bitter against the Parisians who insisted he was a master draftsman but never even mentioned his paintings. He did not want to be a "master draftsman," and felt he had been totally misunderstood. He was to feel this throughout his life, but it was never to stop him from either painting or illustrating. And considering the enormous amount of illustrations he was doing, one is doubly impressed by his ambition and the sheer energy he must have possessed to have produced so much.

Nevertheless, no matter how much Doré may have disliked his reputation as a master draftsman, he never did stop drawing. After *Don Quixote,* his next big project was *The Bible,* which would become known to the next three generations as *The Doré Bible.* It appeared in 1866, at the same time that Gustave Doré fell suddenly and quite madly in love with England and all things English. Much of this love was no doubt due to the reception Doré had received both in America and England. No respectable Victorian parlor, especially those in which both art and religion were revered, lacked a Doré-illustrated volume—more than likely *The Doré Bible.* Moreover the British liked Doré's paintings—especially his great religious paintings—and in 1868, they were exhibited in Egyptian Hall. Shortly afterward, the Doré Gallery was permanently established on Bond Street. The British were delighted, and bought as much of Doré's work as was offered to them. Doré, equally delighted, spent much time in England, painting and drawing as prolifically as always. During the next twenty-one years, great crowds came daily to visit the Doré Gallery to admire his works. After that, the entire gallery was brought over to America, to be exhibited and once again tremendously admired in New York's Carnegie Hall.

Meanwhile, Doré never stopped working. There were more stories to illustrate, more triumphs to win. In 1868–69, he did Tennyson's *Idylls of the King,* then his *London of 1872, The Rhyme of the Ancient Mariner* in 1875, *Orlando Furioso* in 1879, and much other work in between.

In the midst of all this activity, Doré also tried his hand at sculpting and etching, but had no success with either.

In 1881, Doré's beloved Mama died. He was very attached to her, and all of his life she had lived with him, except for a very brief period at the beginning of his stay in Paris. As mentioned earlier, Doré had never really grown up in many ways. He certainly never lost his attachment for his mother, and her death was a great blow. Though he kept on working—even producing two of his most interesting works at this point—things never seemed quite the same again.

Two years later, in 1883 at age fifty, Paul Gustave Doré joined his Mama in death. But it was not the last the public was to hear from him. He had been working on Milton's *Paradise Lost* and Poe's *The Raven*. Published posthumously, *Paradise Lost* took its place in the parlor along with *The Doré Bible*. In fact, like the Bible, this volume was also known as *Doré's Paradise Lost,* for the publishers, thinking it was good business, printed Doré's name in letters far larger than Milton's. They were right, and *Paradise Lost* became, for over two generations, not only a parlor favorite, but possibly the only collection of nudes allowed in a proper household. As for *The Raven,* it was the perfect vehicle for Doré's macabre imagination to play freely for the last time.

Doré's fame and popularity by no means ended with his death. Another three generations were treated to the noted illustrated volumes of stories, myths, and classical literature, and there was probably no aspiring artist who was not influenced by the draftsman. In fact, there is probably no aspiring young artist today who has not or will not feel the strong influence of Doré's work—if he is fortunate enough to see it, for while the drawings have continued to be of special interest to artists, they seem to have had little popular appeal for the last thirty or forty years.

In this selection one has the opportunity to become reacquainted with some of the truly great illustrations of modern times and to recognize the outstanding talent that continues to influence students of draftsmanship.

—JAMES STEVENS

THE BIBLE

THE DELUGE

CAIN AND ABEL OFFERING THEIR SACRIFICES

3

THE DEATH OF ABEL

THE DOVE SENT FORTH FROM THE ARK

ABRAHAM AND THE THREE ANGELS

HAGAR AND ISHMAEL IN THE DESERT

THE BUYERS AND SELLERS DRIVEN OUT OF THE TEMPLE

DANIEL IN THE DEN OF LIONS

THE CROWN OF THORNS

THE CHILDREN DESTROYED BY BEARS

THE ESCAPE OF DAVID THROUGH THE WINDOW

JESUS BLESSING THE CHILDREN

13

MOSES BREAKING THE TABLES OF THE LAW

JESUS WALKING ON THE SEA

THE DEATH OF SAMSON

16

JOB AND HIS FRIENDS

JACOB WRESTLING WITH THE ANGEL

THE CHILD MOSES ON THE NILE

DAVID AND JONATHAN

JACOB GOING INTO EGYPT

ABISHAI SAVING THE LIFE OF DAVID

THE SLAUGHTER OF THE SONS OF ZEDEKIAH

חקל ובָרסין
הנא מנֵא

DANIEL INTERPRETING THE WRITING ON THE WALL

THE VISION OF THE VALLEY OF DRY BONES

25

THE LAST SUPPER

DANIEL

SAINT PETER DELIVERED FROM PRISON

AMOS

MICAH EXHORTING THE ISRAELITES

JESUS HEALING THE SICK MAN OF THE PALSY

ELIJAH NOURISHED BY AN ANGEL

CHRIST MOCKED

33

JEHU'S COMPANIONS FINDING THE REMAINS OF JEZEBEL

THE RESURRECTION OF LAZARUS

SAINT PAUL RESCUED FROM THE MULTITUDE

DEATH OF ATHALIAH

THE VISION OF DEATH

SAINT STEPHEN

EZRA IN PRAYER

THE DEAD CHRIST

THE DESCENT OF THE SPIRIT

JEPHTHAH'S DAUGHTER COMING TO MEET HER FATHER

THE RETURN OF THE ARK TO BETH-SHEMESH

THE JUDGMENT OF SOLOMON

45

THE EGYPTIANS URGE MOSES TO DEPART

BOAZ AND RUTH

THE STRANGE NATIONS SLAIN BY THE LIONS OF SAMARIA

SAMSON DESTROYING THE PHILISTINES WITH THE JAW-BONE OF AN ASS

BABYLON FALLEN

THE ANGEL SHOWING JERUSALEM TO SAINT JOHN

CHRIST AND THE TRIBUTE MONEY

JESUS AND THE WOMAN OF SAMARIA

JESUS FALLING BENEATH THE CROSS

MARY MAGDALENE REPENTANT

THE ERECTION OF THE CROSS

THE RETURN OF THE PRODIGAL SON

ARRIVAL OF THE GOOD SAMARITAN AT THE INN

LAZARUS AT THE RICH MAN'S HOUSE

THE PHARISEE AND THE PUBLICAN

Dante
THE DIVINE COMEDY

"THE INFERNO"
"THE PURGATORIO"
"THE PARADISO"

CHARON, THE FERRYMAN OF HELL

DANTE IN THE GLOOMY WOOD

THE GIANT ANTAEUS

A FLIGHT AND PURSUIT IN HELL

THE PUNISHMENT OF SIMONISTS

THE SPIRIT OF FILIPPO ARGENTI

THE FURIES BEFORE THE GATES OF DIS

THE PUNISHMENT OF FLATTERERS

THE TORTURE OF THE FIERY RAIN

SER BRUNETTO

FARINATA DEGLI UBERTI

THE STYGIAN LAKE

PLUTUS

THE PANTHER IN THE DESERT

BEATRICE AND VIRGIL

PAOLO AND FRANCESCA

THE COMING OF THE BOAT

THE TEMPEST OF HELL

THE TORTURED LOVERS

DANTE AND VIRGIL IN THE HAPPY VALLEY

THE THRESHOLD OF PURGATORY

83

THE MARTYRDOM OF ST. STEPHEN

PIA IN PURGATORY

DANTE'S VISION OF LEAH

DANTE, VIRGIL AND CATO OF UTICA

THE PROCESSION OF THE ELDERS

THE BOAT OF SOULS

DANTE AND THE RIVER OF LETHE

THE PUNISHMENT OF GLUTTONY

DANTE AND POPE ADRIAN V

THE ROMAN WIDOW AND THE EMPEROR TRAJAN

MARCO LOMBARDO

THE PERILOUS PASS

THE SPIRITS OF THE ENVIOUS

A TROOP OF SPIRITS IN PURGATORY

THE BURDEN OF PRIDE

DANTE AND THE EAGLE

THE BREAK OF MORNING

THE ANGELIC GUIDE

DANTE AND THE SPIRITS OF THE MOON

THE ANGELS IN THE PLANET MERCURY

THE VISION OF THE EMPYREAN

THE VISION OF THE SIXTH HEAVEN

THE SPIRITS IN JUPITER

THE VISION OF THE GOLDEN LADDER

THE HEAVENLY CHOIR

THE VISION OF THE CROSS

CHARLES MARTEL

THE SINGING OF THE BLESSED

BEATRICE AND DANTE RISING TO THE FIFTH HEAVEN

THE ANGELIC WREATHS

THE NINTH HEAVEN

DANTE'S ANCESTOR

Milton

PARADISE LOST

SATAN APPROACHING THE CONFINES OF THE EARTH

SATAN AND BEELZEBUB

THE FALLEN ANGELS ON THE WING

SATAN IN COUNCIL

THE REBEL ANGELS SUMMONED TO THE CONCLAVE

SATAN AT THE GATES OF HELL

THE SEVENTH EVENING IN EDEN

THE FIRST APPROACH OF THE SERPENT

125

THE FALL OF THE REBEL ANGELS

SATAN'S FLIGHT THROUGH CHAOS

THE WAR IN HEAVEN

ABDIEL AND SATAN

THE CONFERENCE WITH THE ANGEL RAPHAEL

ITHURIEL AND ZEPHON

SATAN IN PARADISE

THE CREATION OF FISH AND BIRDS

SATAN SMITTEN BY MICHAEL

TIGRIS, AT THE FOOT OF PARADISE

SATAN OVERLOOKING PARADISE

THE COMING OF RAPHAEL

THE BATTLE OF THE ANGELS

THE FALL OF THE REBEL ANGELS

THE RISING OF THE WATERS

ADAM AND EVE

THE EVENING MEAL IN PARADISE

THE MOUTH OF HELL

143

THE GATHERING OF THE WATERS

THE CREATION OF BIRDS

Cervantes

DON QUIXOTE

DON QUIXOTE IN HIS LIBRARY

SANCHO TOSSED IN A BLANKET

THE ANTICS OF DON QUIXOTE

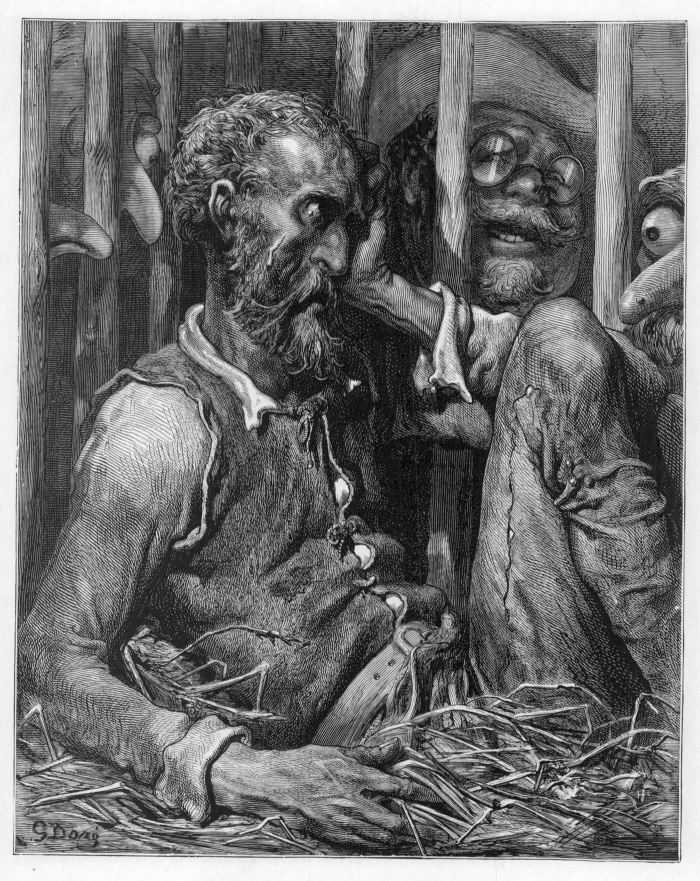

THE ENCHANTMENT OF DON QUIXOTE

THE STEALING OF SANCHO'S ASS

THE ADVENTURE OF THE ENCHANTED BARK

THE MOURNERS FOR DURANDARTE

THE MOCK SERENADE

DON QUIXOTE SETTING OUT ON HIS ADVENTURES

A NOCTURNAL DISCOURSE

DON QUIXOTE'S MADNESS

DON QUIXOTE AND SANCHO SETTING OUT

THE ADVENTURE OF THE FULLING-MILLS

DON QUIXOTE MORALISING ON INGRATITUDE

THE VALIANT CHARGE

H. PISAN

THE BEATEN KNIGHT AND HIS SQUIRE

THE ADVENTURE WITH THE WINDMILLS

THE DON'S MISADVENTURE

THE DON DECEIVED

THE ENCHANTED CASTLE

SANCHO AND THE DUCHESS

Chateaubriand

ATALA

THE WOOD OF BLOOD IN "ATALA"

THE TRIBUTARIES OF THE MISSISSIPPI

THE MISSISSIPPI SAVANNAHS

THE FORESTS ON THE BANKS OF THE MISSISSIPPI

CHACTAS AND ATALA

CHACTAS SEEKING FOR THE GRAVES OF FATHER AUBRY AND ATALA

ATALA AND CHACTAS CROSSING A RIVER

THE BURIAL OF ATALA

THE FIRE IN THE FOREST

THE FALLS OF NIAGARA

THE CAMPFIRE OF ATALA AND CHACTAS

THE BURIAL OF ATALA

THE HERMIT PREACHING IN THE WOODS

THE REST IN THE FOREST

THE NIAGARA ABOVE THE FALLS

THE DEEP MID-FOREST

THE BURIAL-GROUND IN THE FIR-FOREST

THE TOILET IN THE DESERT

SCENERY ON THE MISSISSIPPI

CHACTAS A CAPTIVE

THE LOVERS IN THE MOONLIT FOREST

THE STORM IN THE FOREST

THE HERMIT ON THE MOUNTAIN

MOURNING BY MOONLIGHT

THE VIGIL BY THE GRAVE

THE INDIAN MOTHER AND HER DEAD CHILD

La Fontaine

FABLES

THE VULTURES AND THE PIGEONS

THE GRASSHOPPER AND THE ANT

199

THE HEN WITH THE GOLDEN EGGS

FORTUNE AND THE LITTLE CHILD

THE LITTLE FISH AND THE FISHERMAN

THE MONKEY AND THE DOLPHIN

THE PEACOCK COMPLAINING TO JUNO

THE COUNCIL HELD BY THE RATS

THE FOX AND THE GRAPES

THE HARE AND THE FROGS

THE LION AND THE RAT

THE WOLF TURNED SHEPHERD

THE STAG VIEWING HIMSELF IN THE STREAM

THE OLD WOMAN AND HER SERVANTS

THE COUNTRYMAN AND THE SERPENT

TIRCIS AND AMARANTH

THE EAGLE AND THE MAGPIE

THE MILKMAID AND THE MILKPAIL

THE MAIDEN

THE TWO ADVENTURERS AND THE TALISMAN

THE OYSTER AND ITS CLAIMANTS

THE TWO GOATS

BARON MUNCHAUSEN

Raspe

THE ADVENTURES OF
BARON MUNCHAUSEN

A SUBMARINE WORLD

THE DIVIDED HORSE

THE MAD CLOAK

A VOYAGE TO THE MOON

MUNCHAUSEN AMONG THE BRIGANDS

222

A LUCKY ESCAPE

Perrault

FAIRY TALES

THE PRINCESS AND FAIRY SPRITE

PUSS IN BOOTS

THE APPROACH TO THE ENCHANTED PALACE

LITTLE RED RIDING HOOD

THE PALACE OF SLEEP

THE PRINCE APPROACHING THE PALACE OF SLEEP

THE PRINCE IN THE BANQUETING-HALL

THE SEVEN-LEAGUE BOOTS

THE DWELLING OF THE OGRE

THE LIGHT IN THE WOOD

THE DISGUISED WOLF

L'Épine

THE LEGEND OF
CROQUEMITAINE

MITAINE AND ORGHRIS

THE GNARLED MONSTER

THE CORPSE CANDLES

CHARLEMAGNE'S VISION

THE SPARE BED AT THE CROCODILE